NURTURING
COMPASSION

NURTURING COMPASSION

TEACHINGS FROM THE FIRST VISIT TO EUROPE

THE 17TH KARMAPA
Ogyen Trinley Dorje

Translated by
Ringu Tulku Rinpoche
&
Damchö Diana Finnegan

KARMAPA FOUNDATION
EUROPE

Karmapa Foundation Europe.
23, Rue d'Edimbourg
1050, Brussels
Belgium

www.karmapafoundation.eu

ISBN 978-2-930871-00-4

First Edition
Printed using IngramSpark.

Edited by Damchö Diana Finnegan & Annie Dibble

Designed by Paul O'Connor at Judo Design
Cover Image by Francois Henrard

Contents

INTRODUCTION

In 2014, His Holiness the 17th Karmapa, Ogyen Trinley Dorje, fulfilled the long-treasured wishes of his European students when he visited Germany for two weeks in May and June. On this historic occasion, he travelled across Germany, delivering talks in auditoriums filled to capacity, meeting leaders of different faiths and performing his responsibilities as head of a 900-year-old Buddhist lineage.

For many people, the 17th Karmapa's visit was not only a ground-breaking first visit, it was also a homecoming: a return to familiar ground. His predecessor in the Karmapa reincarnation lineage – His Holiness the 16th Karmapa, Rangjung Rigpe Dorje – had played an instrumental role in introducing Europeans to Tibetan Buddhism in the 1970s. During two major tours of Europe, the 16th Karmapa visited a dozen different countries, offering Black Crown ceremonies and spreading seeds of Dharma in the hearts of countless young Europeans. Four decades and quite a few grey hairs later, many of those same students gathered together from all across Europe to listen to the teachings of the 17th Karmapa, thus continuing their relationship with his predecessor, the 16th Gyalwang Karmapa.

The 17th Karmapa also made many new connections throughout this trip, and he particularly reached out to meet young people. His Holiness often speaks about the major global problems that today's younger generation is facing. He does so not only as a major world spiritual leader, but also as a person in his 20s who shares with his own generation the responsibility for addressing those challenges.

His messages on the environment, consumerism and greed and his emphasis on compassion and loving-kindness as universal values resonated strongly with the thousands of people who attended his teachings. As such, the Gyalwang Karmapa spoke straight to the hearts of not only Buddhist practitioners but also the many people in Europe who are committed to a secular approach and recognise the need for greater human wisdom and compassion in the world today.

The order in which his teachings appear in this book varies from the order in which he gave them. As is appropriate when returning to visit family after a long time away, His Holiness the 17th Karmapa first came to stay at his own European seat, the Kamalashila Institute, in the Eifel region of Germany, where he delivered Dharma teachings and conferred empowerments. Only later did he travel to Berlin where he offered public teachings to a wider audience – including many non-Buddhists. Reversing this order, the book starts with the talks that were given in Berlin and aimed at a broader public; it then presents the more traditional Buddhist teachings delivered at the request of the Kamalashila Institute. Following that, the book brings together the teachings given during empowerments granted in both places. His Holiness taught mainly in Tibetan but often switched into English. The teachings have been lightly edited for publication.

Our most grateful thanks go to His Holiness the 17th Gyalwang Karmapa for his inspiring teachings and giving his permission to publish them in English and other European languages. Venerable Damchö Diana Finnegan transcribed, translated and edited the book with the help of Annie Dibble. We owe special thanks to them and to Paul O'Connor for giving it a beautiful design. We thank all who worked to bring this book to its readers. Finally, we are especially indebted to all those institutions and individuals who made it possible for these teachings to take place, firstly by working to bring His Holiness to Europe, then by organising the teaching events and hosting him.

May this book help to nurture compassion in the hearts of all who read it and bring peace and kindness to this world.

Ringu Tulku
PRESIDENT, KARMAPA FOUNDATION EUROPE
18th June, 2015

PART ONE

PUBLIC TALKS
BERLIN

CHAPTER 1

A MEANINGFUL LIFE

First of all, I would like to express my greetings to you all. This is the first time I have been able to visit Europe, something I have been wishing to do for many years. This stage of my journey takes place in Berlin, the capital of Germany, and I am very pleased to be here.

I have been given a weighty topic to speak on today, with a title so long I can hardly even remember it all – 'Ancient Wisdom for a Modern World: Heart Advice for a Meaningful Life'. As formal and impressive as that sounds, I will be focusing during this part of my time in Europe on informal talks, whereas the portion of my trip spent in Kamalashila Institute near Nürburgring in the Eifel region of Germany has been set aside for more formal Dharma topics.

Today's topic – a meaningful life – leads me to think of my very first encounter with Westerners. My connection to the West, and to Europeans, dates from the time I was recognised as the Karmapa, at the age of seven. My first meeting with Europeans took place as I was being brought to Tsurphu Monastery for the first time. Where the valley narrows, just before arriving at the monastery, there is a park, and it was there that I had my first glimpse of Westerners. There were two Europeans in the park at that time, and I found them really strange looking – tall and thin, like aliens. Ever since then I have had a connection with Europeans and other Westerners, and have made friends with many Europeans. I have been wanting to visit them since I was seven years old. Now I am 28 years old, and am able to fulfil the wish I have held for all these years.

The greatest change in my life took place when I was 14 years old, when I decided to try to escape from Tibet to India at the end of 1999. The press had a lot to say about why I made that decision, and published many different reasons for my fleeing Tibet. Some even gave the explanation that I had come to India to collect some important objects and bring them back. But my real intention in coming to India was principally to have the freedom to be able to travel. For many years I had been lodging one petition after another with the Chinese government for permission to travel, with no result. Therefore I made my own decision to leave for India, in order to be able to travel overseas, meet my Dharma friends and engage in Dharma activities.

In setting out from Tibet for India, we had no reasonable certainty that we would succeed, but our faith spurred us on. As you no doubt know, many other Tibetans continue to flee Tibet for India as I did, and it is from their sincere faith and commitment that they draw the strength that enables them to undertake that journey. I told those who were escaping with me, "Today we are leaving for India, but we do not know whether we will actually succeed in reaching there. Nevertheless, if we meet trouble on the way, we should have no regrets. Since we are facing in the right direction, even if we only manage to take a few steps towards India, there will be no cause for regret."

I was born in Tibet and lived the first 14 years of my life there, and have since spent another 14 years in India – in fact it is coming up to 15 years, and I am only now making my first trip to Europe. During those intervening years, things did not turn out exactly as I had hoped. Although I have lived 28 years so far, which is not a very long time, my life has already been filled with many challenges and changes, and I have gained many different experiences, both good and bad. For this reason, although physically I am young, sometimes I feel as if I am old mentally. I feel as though I have seen enough, and have already become an old man.

This is not the life I chose for myself; it just turned out this way. I did not set out to become the Karmapa nor did I make any effort to receive that name – it simply happened to me. It was not a matter of choice. Apart from that, I have experienced many difficulties: I mention this because it occurs to me that before I talk about a meaningful life, I should be able to say whether or not I find my own life meaningful. Maybe I need to answer first whether I am happy about my own life or not. That is a difficult question. A meaningful life is not something that just comes about without any causes or conditions. It requires effort. Just the fact of being Karmapa does not automatically make life meaningful.

Many people seem to assume that being given the name of Karmapa entails suddenly being endowed with superpowers – as if an alien came from outer space and transported me to a new level. People have the expectation that by virtue of becoming the Karmapa I instantly became powerful, whereas in actual fact I have had to engage in a great deal of study and effort. Before I make any progress, people's expectations have already arrived ahead of me, and this becomes an added difficulty for me. Whether or not we endow our lives with meaning depends on our efforts and actions, and primarily on the motivation we generate. It does not just happen by itself.

When I received the name Karmapa, I faced a unique challenge as to whether or not I would have a personal life apart from my life as Karmapa. Normally, people have a professional life that takes place while they are working, and alongside that they have a personal life that they live when they are not working. For example, someone who works in a factory has a job title that defines what he or she does while on duty. But in my case, for 24 hours a day I am on duty as the Karmapa. Imagine that if you are alone, you are the Karmapa. If you are with others, you are also the Karmapa.

In a way, everything I have must be given over to being the Karmapa. There is no personal life for me outside of being Karmapa. Such things as personal choice, personal freedom, personal rights and a personal life are all out of the question.

If someone asks me, "What is your name?" I have to answer, "Karmapa." If they then ask, "What work do you do?" I also answer, "Karmapa." If they just ask, "Who are you?" I answer, "Karmapa."

This actually happened to me when I first arrived in India as a refugee. For my identity papers, I had to give my name and state my profession. There arose a debate as to whether Karmapa was my name or my title. I could not say Karmapa was not my job title, nor could I say I was not the Karmapa. For several weeks, there were serious debates as to whether Karmapa is a name or a title, and I understand that the discussion was taken up within the Indian government at fairly high levels. The suggestion that it was my job or career to serve as Karmapa but that I was not myself Karmapa sounded pretty good to me. It would mean I was free. In reality, though, that is not how it works. In my own experience, there can be no separation between my personal life and my life as Karmapa, and therefore I have no choice but to work towards living the life of a Karmapa.

'Karmapa' means someone, any woman or man, who engages in the activity of a buddha. The name Karmapa itself contains the word 'karma', which means action in Sanskrit, the ancient language of India. The 'pa' comes from Tibetan and refers to a person. Ideally, a Karmapa is a person of action. At the other end of the spectrum, the Karmapa is a labourer, a kind of servant. The essence of the life of a Karmapa is to work or act to benefit others. If I am able to benefit others, my life as Karmapa becomes meaningful. If I am not able to benefit others, my life as Karmapa is a failure. Therefore my personal life or my life as Karmapa is oriented towards benefitting others. My responsibility – or my life as a Karmapa – is to work to benefit others, based on the Buddha's love and wisdom, lessening and eliminating the suffering of beings and increasing their happiness.

For this reason, it is clear that my life is totally dependent upon others. I truly feel this way. For example, now that I have come to Europe, many people have gathered here. I can see how happy people are about this. I look out at the audience and many faces are smiling back at me. Seeing this I am happy and feel that my life has become meaningful. When I left Tibet, I left behind my parents and gave up all that was familiar to me. But being here in Europe now makes me feel that my sacrifices and efforts were not in vain, but have been meaningful. My life gains meaning entirely through others. By making my life meaningful in this way, other people are being extremely kind to me.

At the bottom of my heart, I always think that my strength comes from others – from people like you – because you give me great hope and aspiration. Even though I may face many challenges, your hope and trust are what has allowed me to survive and carry on, and have made me stronger and able to endure more. The more hope and trust others have in me, the more strength I naturally gain to keep going. The Karmapa's activity and my actions are directed towards benefitting sentient beings, but at the same time the source of the strength to benefit them comes from the sentient beings themselves. Therefore others give meaning to my life.

However, if the question is whether or not my life is a happy one, that is difficult to answer. To speak frankly, my life was happiest before I was recognised as Karmapa. When I was six years old or younger, running around on the grass where I grew up – that was the time when I experienced the most feelings of happiness. Nowadays, I would not say I am very happy. But then, a meaningful life goes much deeper than a feeling of happiness. We need something that lasts beyond temporary states of exhilaration and the emotional excitement that fades after a few moments or a few hours. For life to be meaningful, we need it to bear fruit and to be significant, 24 hours a day, even while we are sleeping.

My point in saying this is that for our life to have meaning, first we need a purpose, and this purpose should be long-term and enduring. It should not be aimed solely at the immediate future, nor should the purpose of our life be selfish. Our lives are interdependent. Our happiness arises through our interdependence with others, as does our suffering. Therefore, since our lives depend on one another, a meaningful life requires that we feel concern for others.

I often think that we might not find value and purpose within the life we live with this one body, but we will find it through others and their lives. In this way, other people become the mirror in which we can see our own dignity and value reflected.

CHAPTER 2

LOVING-KINDNESS

For me being here is like an impossible dream that has come true, and I am very pleased about this. The fact that we have gathered here is important for me, and is the result of a great deal of hardship, so I see this as a precious and special time.

The topic at hand is loving-kindness, and as human beings, we are especially dependent from birth on our parents' love and affection. We also grow based on their love and care. Therefore, from the moment we are born into this world, loving-kindness is indispensable to our very survival.

First of all, our parents give us this body of flesh and bones, and this is an important gift; but their gift of love and affection is even more important. In fact, it is their greatest gift to us. Nevertheless, there are some parents who are not able to show that affection, or give that care, to their children. As a result, such children grow up without a sense of well-being and as adults may be lacking in affection themselves, or experience sadness, loneliness or anxiety.

I was fortunate to be born to kind parents. Not only did my mother and father show love and affection towards me, they also taught me to be loving towards others. I consider my parents to be my first spiritual masters, because what I first learned about loving-kindness I learnt from them. From a very young age, my parents taught me and my siblings to treasure every living being, even a tiny ant, as if they were our very own parents. In this way, my siblings and I were trained to feel affection and respect, and to value the life of all sentient beings. This is something our parents actively taught us.

Thanks to their kindness, right from an early age I formed the predisposition to feel a sense of responsibility to care for others and to find ways to ease their suffering. I feel this was the starting point – and the very best starting point – for my spiritual journey in this life.

My parents are people with single-pointed faith in the Dharma but little intellectual grounding in it. My father knew how to read, but my mother did not. They did not have much formal education, much less any education in Buddhist philosophy. Nevertheless what they taught me they taught from the heart. They did not provide any formal reasoning, but simply offered me a sincere example of how to actually live loving-kindness. This is what touched me deeply.

For this reason, when it comes to training the mind in loving-kindness and compassion, I am not convinced that presenting it through extensive philosophical argument is the most effective method. In one way it is good to know the logical reasoning, but sometimes this just leads us to lose sight of the key points, and gives rise instead to unnecessary doubts. We have a saying in Tibetan to the effect that intellectual exercise can have the result that you accumulate more thoughts, but not more wisdom. As a result, sometimes people who are supposed to be very knowledgeable cannot undo the tough knots they encounter when they grapple with the essential points in actual practice. Instead they approach situations with too many conceptual thoughts, and the knot of doubts can just get tighter and tighter.

I believe that we are all born with loving-kindness and affection as natural human qualities. There can be a difference of degree – some have more and others less – but it is definitely present in all of us. However, our loving-kindness undergoes changes, due to circumstance and to the environment in which we are raised. Sometimes compassion is enhanced, but in other cases it is weakened.

I would like to share an experience from my own life. This took place when I was quite young – maybe three or four – and I still recall it vividly. I was born into a family of nomads, and so we subsisted almost entirely on what we obtained from animals – butter, cheese and meat. Where I was raised, there were no vegetables – no potatoes or anything like that. We had no choice but to rely on our animals.

Autumn was the season for slaughtering livestock, mainly sheep and yak. The main way of slaughtering animals in that area was to bind their muzzles to suffocate them. This was horrible. It took them an hour or so to die. As they struggled to breathe, their distress was terribly evident as their bodies flailed about. They moaned and cried, and would sweat profusely as they died. This was unbearable for me. The wish to protect them, to free them, was so intense that I would cry out, and people used to have to hold me back. The feeling was very strong. This is what happened when the animals were slaughtered.

Yet, despite making such a scene during the slaughter, once the animals had been skinned and the time came to eat the meat, I would be there for the meal, eating as much meat as everyone else, if not more. This was not something that occurred just once, but annually, and after a while, it began to seem that my compassion and affection were pointless. Under those circumstances, my compassion and love for the animals became gradually weaker and weaker over time, and so I kept eating meat. It was only after coming to India that I gave up eating meat, and my main reason for doing so was my recollection of the strong feelings I had when I was young.

Actually, when people ask me what my favourite food is, to be very frank, I would have to say meat. However, since I have given up meat and let go of it completely, there is no longer any food that is a particular favourite.

From the time we are small, we naturally feel affection for others – for dogs, birds or other children. Even when there are no other people or animals around, little children hold on to stuffed animals and dolls, and caress them and take care of them. They have a natural loving quality, treating other people and things with great tenderness and affection. When we are children, we all have this natural capacity for closeness and affection to people and to things. We should take this same spontaneous sense of caring and treasuring, and train ourselves to direct it more and more widely, so that it encompasses all beings without distinction. We should enhance it until it arises effortlessly within us. In this way we can extend and improve our naturally-present quality of loving-kindness. It is very important that we do this.

In short, we all have the natural seeds of love and compassion, but just as we would nurture and protect a sapling until it has developed into a strong tree, we also need to put active efforts into nurturing our love and compassion so that they grow stronger. Throughout the world, and especially in this great nation of Germany, there is a history of inflicting great pain on other peoples due to a lack of loving-kindness. The many terrible situations that arose during the First and Second World Wars, and the Jewish Holocaust, came about primarily due to a lack of compassion. It is not the case that people were not capable of feeling compassion or loving-kindness. We all have this ability from birth. But it definitely seems that our compassion can be switched on and off.

For example, we often say, "That's not my problem. It's their business. It has nothing to do with me." As long as we ourselves or our immediate friends and family are not affected, we do not care what happens to others. In this way, we exclude others from our compassion and just leave them to their own devices, and so slowly we end up lacking in compassion, or becoming cruel and heartless.

When we identify world-killers, we usually single out poverty, pollution, natural disasters, lack of clean drinking water or diseases such as malaria. I feel that our own lack of compassion and loving-kindness is certainly a major world-killer. Many of the situations where people are killed or left in terrible states could be resolved if we just had a bit more compassion. Many people are suffering through our lack of compassion. We can find many examples of this in history.

Just as when we were very young we ourselves needed to receive loving-kindness in our lives in order to survive, I believe it is absolutely indispensable for the world that we connect to others with compassion and love. Humanity cannot do without this.

If someone were to ask us whether we would like to be a world-killer, I doubt any one of us would say yes. However, though it was not our conscious intention, we turn into world-killers, unknowingly and unthinkingly. How does this happen? In our selfishness we think exclusively of ourselves and of our own interests, and in this way we automatically turn into world-killers. This is terrifying.

However, when I speak of the urgent need to cultivate compassion, I do not mean to put pressure on you, or frighten you with the thought that you have become some sort of murderer. We cannot be scared into doing authentic practice. The wish has to arise within us to develop what we already have naturally.

To offer a parable: There was an elderly couple that had only one child, a son, who got into trouble and landed in prison. The parents fell gravely ill with worry, and had no-one to care for them. They could not count on their son. He was stuck in gaol and was unable to get out to look after them. In our selfishness, we are exactly the same. We are trapped in a prison – a gaol of our own making, where no-one but ourselves has placed us. Outside this prison are all other beings, who are like parents to us, but from whom we are separated and disconnected.

These beings need you. They are waiting for you. Yet since you are stuck in this prison of selfishness, you cannot extend yourself out to them. Therefore it is your responsibility, for the sake of those you feel love for, to generate strong compassion and – drawing on the strength it gives you – break out of the prison of selfishness.

CHAPTER 3

THE ENVIRONMENTAL CRISIS

Here in Europe you probably have more information about the environment available to you than I do, so I will have little new to offer in that regard. Nevertheless the environmental crisis is the greatest challenge facing us in the 21st century, in my view. Over the past few years I have given some attention to this issue, and have taken a few small steps towards working to protect the environment.

I sought to educate myself, and then began to speak out on certain environmental issues, convening conferences and undertaking measures in areas such as wildlife and forest conservation. We created an association called Khoryug that links fifty-five monasteries and nunneries in India, Nepal and Bhutan, across the Himalayan region. This association was not limited to monasteries of the Kagyu school of Tibetan Buddhism but included various lineages. We established a dedicated wing within each monastery and nunnery, and launched a campaign to increase environmental awareness and action, not only within each monastery but also across their affiliated institutions. I thought it was important for the monks and nuns to gain a sound understanding of environmental issues, since monastics serve as leaders in Himalayan communities. This has been going on for several years now.

The glaciers and ice cover of the Himalayas and the Tibetan plateau serve as the source of so many of Asia's rivers that the

Tibetan plateau is known as 'Asia's water tower'. Scientists have begun referring to it as the world's Third Pole for this same reason. It is in Tibet in particular that a great many of Asia's major rivers have their point of origin, which makes the Tibetan plateau a crucial life-giving force for the natural environment of the planet generally and Asia in particular.

Because of this, I saw it as especially important for the people of the Himalayas to gain awareness of environmental issues. Although in the past their way of life was in harmony with the natural environment, this is no longer the case. Nowadays, due to the rapid material development that has taken place, the way of life has changed and many people are unaware of the ways in which their new lifestyle and material development harm the environment. They do not realise that plastics do not biodegrade but last for thousands of years, therefore they just leave them on the ground wherever it suits them. Previously it never occurred to them to make any special or conscious effort to protect the environment, because their way of life had evolved in harmony with their natural surroundings.

When people hear of the 'Tibetan issue', immediately what comes to mind for many is 'politics'. However, in my view, the Tibetan issue does not necessarily need to be seen as an entirely political issue. For example, the issue of the Tibetan environment is not a political issue. It is not even a matter of concern solely for Tibetans, nor for any single country. The issue of the Tibetan natural environment is an issue for all of Asia. Indeed, looking at the broader context, it is an issue that concerns the entire planet. From this wider angle we can see that the Tibetan people had lived in harmony for thousands of years with the natural environment of the Tibetan plateau. Therefore in order to protect that Tibetan environment, there is a need to protect the Tibetan way of life: the Tibetan culture, spiritual traditions, habits and ways of thinking which are compatible with and suited to that environment. This is beyond politics. It goes beyond the interests of any single race or any single nation.

Although I do have an interest in environmental matters, I am not knowledgeable or experienced myself. However, I have had the support of the World Wildlife Fund (WWF), and in particular a woman from WWF who has taken responsibility for my environmental activities.

To be moved by environmental issues and to see the necessity for acting on them, some image needs to arise in our mind when we hear about the environment. Nowadays many people have moved to cities. People raised in urban settings lack close contact with nature. The beauty of nature is something they increasingly only see by looking at a photo, rather than by growing up within the natural world, experiencing its beauty and directly witnessing its importance and necessity. In my own case I was fortunate to be raised in the wilderness of eastern Tibet, in an area completely untouched by modern development. Our way of life was exactly the same way of life that had been lived there for thousands of years, utterly unchanged and unaffected.

Nowadays, the opportunity to experience that is gone. It has all been modernised. But at that time, it was still possible, and I had the opportunity to be close to nature and to gain experience of the traditional way of life compatible with that natural environment. Therefore I carry within me a strong basis that allows me to appreciate the tremendous importance of the environment, and to have a real feeling of love, care and respect for nature. I think perhaps that is why, when I talk about the environment, I am not just expressing concepts, but do have some real feeling and connection to it, and can speak from that.

There is a tendency these days to look at results, but not see their causes. For example, in the supermarket one sees displays of packaged beef, chicken and other types of meat. Many children have the impression that meat is produced in the supermarket, and have little awareness that it involves raising animals, inflicting great distress and pain on them, and, in the end, slaughtering them. We do not see the causes and conditions, but just see packaged meat that looks like something produced in a factory.

The preceding causes and conditions appear to be very distant from the results we see right in front of us. Similarly in the case of the natural environment, if the changes that take place and the problems caused by environmental degradation are far away, we do not see them and do not understand them.

As I mentioned, I have no great knowledge about the environment. However, I can say that in the final analysis, the environmental issue is an issue of the mind, because it comes down to human conduct, and what drives our conduct is our motivation, or our intentions and attitudes. This is why I say the destruction of the natural environment comes from human desires and human greed.

To understand how desire works, Buddhism offers the analogy of a silkworm that spins threads of silk to create a cocoon within which the silkworm itself gets trapped. In exactly this way, desire keeps producing more desire. Through our desire, we trap ourselves in our own webs. Desire never brings an end to desire; it only gives rise to more desire.

Wherever we go nowadays, whether we watch TV or read the newspaper, as we go down the street or look at the mobile phone in our hand, everywhere we encounter something to increase our greed. Advertising constantly encourages us to acquire something else, telling us, "This is good; that is good. Buy this! Buy that!" Most of what we see and hear seems to be designed to create desire and stimulate our greed.

What is the effect of this? Our desires increase. We continually want more things, and so we buy them. What does this do? It places greater pressure on the environment, which is our source for all the natural resources required to manufacture these products. We do not just exploit the environment; we over-exploit it. Therefore, if we ask what the real cause of the environmental degradation is, I think we must say it comes down to the desire and greed in human minds and hearts.

But if we ask whether or not there is an end to human desire, or whether there will come a time when our desires are satisfied, I think that this is very unlikely. In this age of materialism, corporations and governments promise to satisfy all our desires, yet they are praying that our desires will increase. Our prayer is, "May we be free of desire," while they are praying, "May they have more desire!" They pray and they also apply all the means at their disposal to stimulate our desire. At the same time they promise that we will be able to continue with our current lifestyle and will not need to make any real changes. It is similar to when presidential candidates running for office make many different promises: "Not to worry; I'll do this. I'll do that. I promise."

In this way we close our eyes to actual reality and live our lives instead in a world of illusion. Human beings do not actually have huge stomachs, but mentally our stomachs seem huge. You could fit three planets the size of this earth into the stomach of our mind.

What can we do about this? We need to realise that our thirst for material things can never be quenched. Once we see that our desires are simply unquenchable, we must ask whether there is any other way. If there is, then we must pursue it.

If I were running for president, I suspect I would not get many votes. People would think, "He keeps telling us we have to change, that this isn't going to work and that our desires cannot be fulfilled." They would expect me to promise and guarantee that I will take care of everything and that they do not need to do anything or change anything. I would not be a very successful candidate.

Yesterday I went to an Italian restaurant, and was served a huge pizza. Sometimes I think a whole pizza is too much for our stomachs, and we might not actually need such a big meal. But in terms of our wants, even a pizza that we cannot eat is not enough. What we want is to have the whole planet earth, and even then we would not be satisfied. Therefore I think we must differentiate clearly between what we want and what we need. It is crucial that we understand the difference between the two.

This is not to say that we must learn to do without any material resources at all. That would be going too far. We do need some material resources. We do not all need to live like Milarepa. That would be too extreme and it is not fitting for everyone, nor is it necessary. But we do need to find a balance between our inner, mental resources and our outer, material resources. How we can begin to do this is by looking at what we do have and trying to feel satisfied and content with that.

In my experience, we look down on what is ordinary and simple and are not content with it. We have the constant expectation that things should be better and more fancy, and we make things more complicated. However, in actual reality what makes us happy is simple and ordinary, in my view.

For example, it can be just breathing. Breathing is very ordinary and nothing special. But if we direct our attention to it and savour the experience, we can come to see that the simple act of breathing is absolutely amazing. The oxygen we need must come from outside us, from the plants and trees. We cannot survive without breathing; yet with absolutely no effort on our part, all the conditions we need are continually and naturally present. This is true not just for one breath, but for one after another. This alone can produce a tremendous sense of wonder, satisfaction and happiness.

CHAPTER 4

COMPASSION IN A GLOBALISED WORLD

Ours is the only planet in the universe known to sustain life. We can imagine that there may be others, but this is the only one we have identified thus far. Life on this planet is extremely diverse. We know of a great number of life forms already, and continue to identify new species; even on a single tree we can find many different types of insects. Among all these species, humans represent just one. Within our single species there is likewise great diversity: a diversity of race, a diversity of physical types, and in fact each of us has a unique fingerprint. In short, the biodiversity on this planet is highly varied and complex. The beings of this planet are also diverse in terms of their forms of behaviour as well as their circumstances. Yet in the midst of all this diversity, ultimately we are all mutually dependent and reliant upon one another.

We tend to think that an elephant is more valuable because it is big. If we look at an insect, it can seem insignificant and impotent by comparison. We might think it serves no great purpose, but actually, everything has a purpose, precisely because all life forms on this planet are mutually dependent and mutually supportive, and all form part of the same living system.

For instance, a bee has a tiny body, yet its benefit is great. Bees extract the pollen from flowers, and then fertilise other plants. This is of tremendous benefit to the planet and to human beings, and we are hearing more and more from scientists about the important functions that different species play. The point is that we are all connected. All things on this planet, both animate and inanimate, and especially the living beings, are interrelated and interconnected. They have a connection.

From a Buddhist perspective, we give a name to this sort of relationship – a beautiful and fitting one – namely, the relationship of 'mother and child'. We do not use this phrase in the sense of a relationship between two wholly separate objects, as if there were a mother over here and a child over there. Rather, in this context, the term 'mother and child' primarily indicates that we have a close and positive connection and a sort of shared spirit or potential. Taking the mother-and-child relationship as a model, we can come to gain a clear, positive image of ourselves as having this same intimate connection to the world that surrounds us, in its sentient and non-sentient forms.

We all have an innate sense of self or self-grasping – a sense of autonomy or independence from others. We feel that we can do without others, and hold on to a sense of ourselves as separate from them. Yet if we consider carefully the actual reality and ask whether or not there truly exists any such self-sufficient or autonomous self, we see that what we are mainly taking as a basis for this label 'me' is our body. This physical form that we can perceive serves as the primary point of reference for our sense of an independent self or 'me', yet our body is very clearly not something independent. On the contrary, it depended on our parents to bring it into existence, and, in a more subtle sense, it came from the substances of others. Moreover, just having a body is insufficient. We also need to sustain that body. If we do not have clothes, food and the many other additional resources we need to stay alive, this body becomes nothing but a corpse.

Where do the food and clothing our body depends upon come from? These too come from others. Particularly now in this context of globalisation, much of what we use comes from far away. We eat fruit grown in another country, and wear clothes manufactured in distant parts of the globe. We might live in a developed country, dressed in garments produced by people in an underdeveloped country or impoverished area. We do not see the people who make our clothes, or know them, yet we are wearing clothes that they worked to produce.

To share some of my own personal experience, up to the age of seven I lived like an ordinary person, with a strong feeling of family. Ours was not the sort of family where the father goes off to his job and the mother goes to her job. We were mostly together. In the evenings, we would usually gather in a circle around a fire, and my parents and the older people would tell stories. This gave us a very close family feeling and sense of togetherness.

I was a nomad, as I mentioned, so we relocated often and moved around a lot. We had a great deal of freedom. We children could run anywhere we wanted in the wide-open spaces around us. There was no fear of being hit by a car. Except where we stayed in the winters, there weren't even any buildings anywhere around, and we spent the summers living in a yak-hair tent.

In that way, I grew up experiencing a strong sense of freedom of movement. Then, suddenly, at the age of seven, I parted from my family and went to live far away in a monastery. Tsurphu Monastery has three storeys, and I was put into living quarters on the top floor. I was separated from my family, and my earlier feelings were replaced by new feelings. When that happened I felt something that I could call suffering or unhappiness.

Children need other children of their own age to play with, but when I got to Tsurphu Monastery, there was no-one my age. Everyone around me was old, and not only did they look old, they looked serious. They looked at me as if to say, "I don't want to play with you. What are you doing?"

My point is that after being raised the way I was, I came to see that others could also act as parents or fulfil the role of parents or friends to me. I looked for that. Many people came to see me from around the world. Most of them regarded me as a lama, and so they elevated me and took me very seriously. However, from my point of view, I felt the absence of parents and friends – a kind of emptiness – and was trying to fill that gap. If I looked around, I could see that most of what I had was given to me by others – even the toilet paper, everything. I came to feel that there were always many people taking care of me. Slowly I realised that I did not only have biological parents, but I also had other kinds of parents or friends, who helped me.

When we speak of changing the world from the inside out, this entails cultivating within our minds a strong sense of love and affection, gradually, freely and very comfortably. When we generate compassion in this way, it can be natural and authentic.

Being a Buddhist is not a matter of being obliged to be compassionate, whether you want to or not. There is no high lama issuing you the command, "Meditate on compassion, right now." You might be able to force something, but it is unlikely that it would be heartfelt.

Compassion is more than sympathy and more than empathy. With sympathy and empathy, most of the time there is a sense of placing the object of your sympathy over there and having some understanding of their situation or where they come from. Compassion is deeper and more strongly felt than that. With compassion you do not experience the person as an object over there, separate from you, but rather you have the wish or the feeling that you have become the other. That is the sort of feeling we are aiming for. Compassion has a sense of coming out from where you are, and going over to the position of the other – even jumping across to their position.

In short, compassion makes us a part of others. It brings us out from our own space and moves us into the place of the other.

Compassion is not a matter of staying in our own space, looking down at their suffering and calling ourselves compassionate.

The world today has become smaller, and the connections that bind us together are tighter. More than ever before, the difference between self and other is less than we think it is. What we call 'other' is a part of our self. Who we are, is a part of others. Therefore our happiness and suffering depend on others' happiness and suffering. Others' happiness and suffering are naturally a part of our own happiness and suffering. Our own and others' experiences of pain and joy are interrelated and interdependent, both directly and indirectly. Therefore, as I said earlier, if we are able to see the relationship between ourselves and others, and the whole of our global society, through great love and great compassion and with great courage, this will certainly benefit our own life and will lend great strength to our efforts to benefit others.

CHAPTER 5

ART

I have a great interest in the arts, such as painting, music and theatre. In the case of painting, I not only take an interest: I also feel that I gain strength from it. I think this is because I am a person with many aspirations, ideas and hopes, and yet, although I dream up lots of different projects and plans, I often encounter many obstacles in implementing them. Over time, my enthusiasm for such projects begins to wane. Painting helps, because it is an activity where I can directly bring to fruition whatever it is I wish to see manifest. When I paint, the results are immediately visible, and I feel a strong sense of accomplishment.

Sometimes we have a positive thought and are moved by an altruistic motivation to benefit others, but the response is not what we had hoped for. People might not accept our offer of help. We ourselves might feel our capacity was not adequate to the task, or we might be left with the feeling that our virtue lacked strength. However, when it comes to art, there are no such problems: for example, when children make drawings, they are not concerned about the reactions of grown-ups or other people. They simply express on paper whatever arises spontaneously in their heart or mind, without forcing or faking anything and without worrying whether others will like it or not.

Similarly, when it comes to engaging in virtue, it is important that we do not act to please or impress anyone. Rather, we should be expressing whatever is pure and spontaneous in our heart and mind, without pretence, phoniness or hesitation. First, we

31

bring forth whatever we find within ourselves that is beautiful and spontaneous, and only later do we consider whether it will be accepted or not. Otherwise, sometimes others have strong expectations and we might feel we will not be able to show them what we have that is beautiful. This is the feeling that comes.

CHAPTER 6

MEETING WITH YOUNG PEOPLE

Welcome to all the young people who have come here. I see there are some 'old' young people here as well, so welcome to you, too. This is my first visit to Europe, and being able to meet all you young people is a special opportunity for me. I really enjoy this and want to thank you for coming here.

When I was a young child, I was recognised as the reincarnation of the Karmapa. After that I had little opportunity to be with anyone of my age, or talk to other children or play with them. Most of the people around me were much older than I was. On top of that the Tibetan custom is that lamas do not move much, but sit still like statues. Sometimes I saw other children playing together and going to school, and thought they looked so happy. I used to wish I could join them.

My body is supposed to be young – 28 years old – but from a young age I have had a huge responsibility and faced so many challenges that I have the feeling that my mind has already aged. That makes me a strange kind of young person.

In the 21st century, young people have many pressures. We have pressures from our studies. We are placed under pressure from many directions. The world has become smaller and the pressures have become greater. Development is progressing so swiftly and things are changing so fast that we are always scrambling to catch up, so we can never seem to rest. This is another problem we face.

Moreover, our way of life in this century is so based on material things that we are using up natural resources at a pace that cannot be sustained. We will not be able to continue this lifestyle. Therefore the welfare of future generations is very much connected to us. Whether things work out well for the world or not will be determined by us in this century. In this way, we could say that the young people of today have a responsibility, but we could also say that we have a unique opportunity to create a brighter and more wholesome future for the world.

That future starts now. The future is not a matter of tomorrow or the next day. The future is already starting in this very next second.

Now I think it is time for some questions.

———

Audience: I am 14 years old, from Berlin. I am asking a question for my sister. She is ten years old. Her question is: How do I become a buddha?

Karmapa: 'Buddha' means to blossom, like a flower-bud opening, and it also means to wake up. Becoming a buddha is not about getting superpowers like Superman, or having something injected into your blood or your genes to make you strong. Really it is more about being a good-hearted person. If you give someone a present and make them smile and feel happy, you have become a buddha, a little buddha. Knowing what to do to bring joy to the hearts of others, and doing it – that is what it means to be a buddha.

———

Audience: I am from Berlin, and I am 13 years old. My question is: How do you experience carrying all the responsibilities and people's expectations of being the Karmapa. Is it more an honour or a burden?

Karmapa: Actually, people think the Karmapa does not make any mistakes. They expect the Karmapa to be perfect. That is not possible for me. I cannot think of it that way, so I have another way to view it that makes it easier for me. Instead of thinking about being Karmapa as having authority, I think of it as having an opportunity. It is a big chance to help a lot of people. So I tell myself, "I have been given a big chance. This is a really good opportunity".

———

Audience: Hello, I am 13 years old and I am from Madrid, Spain. My question is: Will the world continue to exist or will it end? What can I do to help the world?

Karmapa: In school, we learn that at one point there was no life on this planet, and then life began. Things developed over a very long time, and at a certain point the human species came into existence. This shows that things change, so it is natural that one day the earth also will come to an end.

The biggest danger for us at this moment is the environmental crisis. If the natural environment of our world is destroyed, the human race will have a very hard time to survive. So working to preserve the environment is very important. It will not just help one person, but will help the whole world. That would be very good.

———

Audience: I am from Austria and I am 26 years old. My question is: How do you see the relationship between religion, spirituality and culture, and which one has the strongest influence?

Karmapa: I think I should do some research! I am not sure whether this will directly answer your question about which is more influential, but I think religion is more like a system of doctrines, traditions and customs. Spirituality is not about tradition, but is mainly rooted in a deeper experience and feeling of life, and in wisdom and compassion. Culture is connected to many other things, so I will leave that aside. I think that all the major religious traditions started as spirituality, rooted in real life experience – not just customs, traditions or a belief system. The Buddha is one example of that. From his childhood, he had big questions about his life: Who am I? What is the meaning of my life and of this world? He was trying to find that meaning and reality, you could say.

For that purpose, he gave up his life as a prince in the palace and went to a solitary place and thought constantly about those questions. In the end, he felt he had somehow discovered the answers. He really appreciated the answers he found, and was satisfied by them. However, the people who later adopted the Buddha's path and his tradition were just following his system or his ideas, without really having that kind of experience for themselves. They just followed along behind. That is why I think religious followers run into certain dangers. Actually religious practitioners should be spiritual, and should have some authentic experience. Rather than artificial belief, they should have real knowledge. However, it is not easy to find those answers, so maybe people take the easy way, and just believe. That is why I think spirituality is more effective than having religious beliefs or faith.

———

Audience: Hello, Karmapa. I am 22 years old. I am a Taiwanese-Canadian from Halifax, Canada. My question is: A lot of young people, myself included, take too many things in life for granted – rights, freedom, safety, parents, caring and forgiveness. How can we increase our awareness when selfish thoughts arise so that we can eliminate them and nurture a long-term appreciation for others?

Karmapa: This is an important point. In developed countries, many facilities have already been created for us. Our parents also brought together the conditions for us to receive a good education and to have lots of good opportunities. It is important to feel appreciation or gratitude.

There are many children in the world who do not have such opportunities to receive an education, or who do not have enough to eat, or, have no access to clean water or health care. We must think about them. We should not always be setting our expectations by comparing ourselves to those who have more than us.

If you compare yourself to others who are in more difficult situations and have greater problems, then you can recognise how well off you are. But recognising that you are fortunate should not make you feel superior or proud. Rather, it should make you think, "Oh, I have a responsibility. Because I was given these opportunities in life, I must make good use of them so that in the future I will be able to help other young people who did not have the same chances as I did".

Gratitude is important because it brings you satisfaction and joy naturally, without your needing to do anything else. That is the power of gratitude.

———

Audience: Good afternoon, Your Holiness. I just have a simple question: How do we practise contentment or satisfaction, and at the same time, progress in our lives?

Karmapa: I do not think there is any contradiction between feeling contented and progressing in life. Contentment is the ability to enjoy fully what you have. Contentment does not mean that you stop progressing. It means being able to savour and make full use of what you have.

There is a saying in Buddhism that when you are engaging in virtuous actions, you should not be like a rich person, but like a beggar. Somehow it is not appropriate to have the attitude of a rich person with lots of money who buys a big house and a fancy car. The outlook we should have when we are doing something virtuous is that of a beggar who does not have much money. Let's say a beggar gets a small amount of money, like one euro. Actually, I should not call that 'small' as that would not be a small amount of money in India! So let's say a beggar obtains ten euros. That is an amount that a beggar would really be able to value. Obtaining it, he feels something special, and is overjoyed, and can fully savour and experience the flavour of that joy. Being satisfied or contented does not mean we refuse to receive more. It means truly appreciating what we have.

We can take an iPhone as an example. Nowadays iPhones are everywhere in the world: iPhone 4 and 5, and I guess 6 must be coming soon. We are waiting for iPhone 6! Whenever something new comes, we have to rush out and buy it. Yet we do not even make full use of the older version we have. If we do not know how to use all the features of the iPhone 5, but still buy a later version of the iPhone, there is not much difference. It might have a slightly different design and be slightly thinner, but in reality if we are not even using all the features of the iPhone 5, then getting an iPhone 6 pretty much means just getting more of the same.

That is why we need to know how to fully appreciate and recognise the value of what we have now. That does not mean we have to stop there and will not get more. We do need to progress, but we should progress with recognition and appreciation, so that our progress is not just ignorant progress.

———

Audience: Hello, I am 23 years old, from Austria. My question is: My grandmother, who is old and sick, seems to be getting closer and closer to dying, and I wonder what I can do to help her face death. Also, when she is dying, what would be the most helpful thing for her to do?

Karmapa: The most important thing is to learn to accept death. Sometimes we human beings are so selfish and so full of ourselves that we want to be exempt from nature. Death is natural. It is a natural process of change. If we were born, we are going to die. Yet we humans are so arrogant that we think we should be beyond the cycle of life and death. We are not. In fact, thinking this way just increases our suffering. Therefore we should accept death. This is very important.

We celebrate our birthday, but that is actually like celebrating our death. It is because you were born that you will die.

In order to learn to accept death, though, we need some training. There are many exercises and different ways to train in this. One way is that you think of one day as one life. When you wake up in your bed, it is like being born. Then you slowly grow up, and at night when you go to sleep, it is like dying.

With this kind of training you will naturally come to accept death. It is something that happens every day, so it is not as if each of these deaths is really final. Every day you have this lesson or training, until one day you get to the point that you can accept death. When your real death comes, you will see it as somewhat similar to these many small deaths you have been experiencing each day. You will be able to see it as something familiar. It will not be anything you need to worry about or to fear. It will just be like going to sleep.

———

Audience: Hello, I am 20 years old and I come from Austria. My question is: Sometimes I have phases when certain fears and anxieties recur again and again, and I experience a strange attachment to them. I cannot let go of them. The fear itself is not the main problem, but the fact that it returns again and again in my mind. Can you give advice on how to overcome such a situation in a good and effective way? Thank you very much.

Karmapa: This is not an easy question. Anxiety often comes when we are unfamiliar with something and have no experience of it. When the fear or anxiety arises, you can imagine that it becomes Chenrezig or Tara, or your mother or someone you feel comfortable with, or white light. I think that will help. Then you can meditate on that image. That might make it easier for you.

———

PART TWO

DHARMA
TEACHINGS
NÜRBURGRING

CHAPTER 7

Ngöndro I: The Common Preliminary Practices

I have been asked to speak about *ngöndro*, which is a traditional, formal Dharma topic. The ngöndro, or preliminary practices, are divided into two stages, the common preliminary practices and the special preliminary practices. The common preliminary practices are also called The Four Thoughts that Turn the Mind to Dharma. These four comprise 'precious human life', 'death and impermanence', 'karma' and 'the defects of samsara'.

The common ngöndro begins with the contemplation of the preciousness of human life. This contemplation is important and necessary for all human beings who seek to make their lives meaningful, whether long-time practitioners of Buddhism, newcomers to Buddhism or non-Buddhists.

Contemplating the fact that our precious human life is difficult to attain and easily lost helps us to recognise that in this moment we have all the conditions that are propitious for the practice of Dharma and are free of all conditions adverse to it. In this case, 'Dharma' does not necessarily refer to some sort of religious practice, but can be taken to mean striving to be a good human being – someone who is compassionate and non-violent and who engages in positive actions and intentions. That, too, is practising Dharma.

The teaching on precious human life shows us that this human body of ours has the potential to allow us to accomplish significant and vast things, not only for ourselves, but for many others. It points out just what an opportunity this human body represents. All human beings are fundamentally endowed with love, compassion and other positive qualities, not as products of religious practice, but as something present within us all right from birth. The most important thing, and the basis of Dharma practice, is for us to value these innate human qualities, and work to enhance and develop them.

Therefore, to be a Dharma practitioner does not imply becoming someone different. There is no need to become a strange or new person. Nor are we necessarily adopting a whole new lifestyle. Rather, we are bringing out the natural qualities inherent in us, within the life we are already leading. For this reason, Dharma practice is not something we do apart from, or outside of, our ordinary life.

For example, let's say we have decided to practise Dharma. We may be confident that we are a Buddhist practitioner, but if pressed to say whether we are a good person, we are not certain. Sometimes we are sort of a good person, sometimes not so much. This is inadequate. We cannot be good Dharma practitioners without striving to become good human beings. This underscores the need for our Dharma practice to take place within our life, not outside of it. Practising Dharma means transforming ourselves and enhancing the positive qualities we possess. This is a key point.

Being human brings with it the opportunity to become a better human being, and that opportunity also represents a responsibility. If I can share my own personal experiences: I lived like any ordinary boy up to the age of seven years, when I was recognised as the reincarnation of Karmapa. However, as I have mentioned, simply being given the name 'Karmapa' did not imply being injected or fed some special substance that imbued me with special powers. I needed to study hard and practise.

Since I was Karmapa, many people connected to the Karmapa came to see me, bringing their great hopes and expectations of me and placing their trust in me. Initially, when I had first been told that I was the Karmapa, it was like a game to me. At first I did not see it as anything particularly serious. Only gradually did I come to realise that there are responsibilities that come with the name Karmapa.

Yet we all have responsibilities. We have responsibilities towards ourselves. We have responsibilities towards our families and, in the broadest terms, we have responsibilities towards the whole world. In my own case, I was especially alerted to my responsibilities by the fact that I was given the name Karmapa. But apart from that, we are all basically the same. It is mainly a matter of whether or not our responsibilities are made clear to us.

However, we have such strong habits of selfishness that we ignore the fact that we have these responsibilities, or we lack sufficient courage and confidence to assume them. I too sometimes suffer from the problem that my responsibilities begin to feel like a form of pressure, or a heavy burden that is difficult to carry. Why do we feel this sense of pressure? I think it is a lack of love and compassion. In my view, it is because our compassion lacks strength, and the element of courage or confidence, that we experience our responsibilities as a burden. Therefore it is very important to increase the strength of our compassion.

This brings us back to the topic of the preciousness of our human life: although our human body has immense value, in order to be able to assume the responsibility for making full use of that value, we definitely need the power of compassion and courage. This will allow us to live our lives in a meaningful way.

Having a precious human life allows us to accomplish great things. As I have said, I believe that everyone is innately endowed with the power of compassion. Yet in our selfishness we find excuses for shutting the door on it. The great natural potential we have gets enclosed within our selfishness. When we fall under the sway of our self-centredness, our environment closes in on us. Our selfishness traps us in a kind of prison. We become unable to extend our innate potential beyond the walls of that prison. This is why it is so important to enhance the strength of our love, our compassion and our altruistic intentions. Doing so will allow us to emerge from that prison, bringing forth our natural potential and our full capacity to benefit others. We will be able to fulfil the great purpose of our life, and make our human life fully meaningful.

In Europe and the West generally, it is considered very important to protect one's individual rights, personal freedom and interests. These should not become mixed with selfishness, and I believe there is a danger that the two do become mixed. For that reason, we need to ensure that we are able to distinguish correctly between selfishness, on the one hand, and the protection of individual rights, personal freedom and interests, on the other.

To that end, it is very important to understand what is meant by 'self'. There is a vast difference between actual reality and how the self appears to us. We assume that how things appear to us or how we experience them is how they really are. But, ultimately, there is a distinction between appearances and reality. Many people normally have a feeling that the self – or what we refer to when we say "I" – is something self-sufficient and not dependent on others. However, in reality, if we think about it, our very body, from our head to our toes, arises entirely based on others. Our ability to survive is thoroughly dependent upon others. The food we eat, the clothes we wear, even the air we breathe – this all comes from others. This is perfectly obvious.

There is nothing wrong with feeling that we have a self, but we need to ask what kind of a self exists. What is this 'I' that exists? We must question whether it is singular and independent, as we usually assume. That kind of 'I' in reality does not exist. But sometimes we can make up reality. It is not reality, but we think that it is. This is why we should have a very clear understanding of how this 'I' exists. We need to examine carefully so that we see that in actual fact, our self is utterly interdependent on others, and is in no way independent or unrelated to anything else. It is not that 'I' do not exist. We do exist, but we need to understand *how* we exist. When we see that we exist as an interdependent arising, in mutual dependence on others, then without a doubt we will feel a sense of responsibility for others. This is why I feel that interdependence is not just a philosophical view, but a value or a way of life.

If we have this awareness of our self as arising interdependently, then, when we consider all the resources we enjoy that come from the natural environment, we see how thoroughly we rely on it. From that awareness, a sense of concern and care will definitely arise, naturally. We will naturally think of protecting the environment. This is how a sense of responsibility is supported by an awareness of interdependence and of the preciousness of our human life.

Among the four thoughts that turn the mind to Dharma, or 'four common preliminary practices', the topic that follows 'precious human life' is 'the impermanence of life'. We usually describe this as 'death and impermanence', but today I do not want to talk about death!

From the time we are born, we undergo enormous changes throughout our life. Our body changes tremendously. Mentally we change a great deal. There are many changes that take place in our surrounding environment, and there is no stopping this process of change. We did not intentionally set out to make things change; it just happens, naturally. What impermanence means is that it is natural for things to change. Nothing stays the same.

Why do we need to contemplate impermanence? The fact that things change does not mean we lose something. Rather, it is a sign that we have new opportunities and new options. We meditate on impermanence in order to see that the change that takes place moment to moment represents moment after moment of opportunity. The opportunities available to us are inexhaustible and limitless, and are arising continuously. We meditate on impermanence so that we can make full use of these opportunities and make good choices.

Many people have difficult experiences in childhood, and never rid themselves of these bad memories. Instead, they internalise them, and are pained and oppressed by them throughout their lives. There are also people who have themselves done something terrible, and carry such guilt that they never get over it. Engaging in the practice of contemplating impermanence shows us that we can make a fresh start in life at any time. A new light can dawn for us. We do not need to continue on the same trajectory. Just because a particular situation arose in the past does not mean we need to keep living out that storyline. We can begin a new chapter, a new story and a new life.

For instance, if a person with a strong practice of contemplating impermanence has only five minutes left to live, they will try to make those five minutes meaningful. Making those last five minutes meaningful can effectively make their entire life meaningful.

Life is something to be greatly cherished. It unfolds from moment to moment. Meditating on death and impermanence makes us aware of that fact, and teaches us to cherish each and every moment of our lives. If we make just one moment meaningful, that amounts to the same thing as making our whole life greatly meaningful. Our life is taking place in each moment.

Sometimes people think the traditional meditation on death and impermanence involves having the painful and frightening thought, "I am going to die! Oh, no!" That is not a correct understanding of what contemplating impermanence means. Rather, it means not letting even a tiny part of our life go to waste. By cherishing our life and earnestly applying ourselves to living it fully, we are accomplishing the purpose of meditating on death and impermanence.

Within the four thoughts that turn the mind to Dharma, there is some flexibility in the order in which the last two topics – 'karma' and 'the defects of samsara' – are presented. But to take karma next, it could be described as cause and effect, as karmic connections, as the law of karmic causality or just as karma. In any case, I believe the word 'karma' now appears in the dictionaries of many Western languages. It can be challenging to explain what karma means, because the workings of karma are beyond our conception. For this reason, we generally find it to be a complicated and difficult concept. Yet I do not feel it needs to be complicated or confusing.

When I first arrived in Germany, I landed in Frankfurt. As the plane was descending, I was struck by how green everything was. The trees looked shiny and healthy to me. This is an indication that the people inhabiting the area care for the environment, and are aware of its importance. No one needs to explain that it is because someone has previously cared for the environment that we now see this result – it is immediately apparent to any observer, even to a complete newcomer like me.

Karma works in a similar way. To give an example, if someone plants a seed, provides all the necessary conditions, and wards off any adverse conditions, then at the end of that process they will be able to see a beautiful tree. That is how karmic cause and effect works. We can see that actions motivated by a positive, virtuous intention to protect that environment have tangible results, and this shows us that our motivation has great influence and power. Any action very much depends on the motivation and purpose of the person engaging in it. Thus in whatever we do, we should act assuming proper responsibility and paying careful attention to karmic causes and their results.

Karmic cause and effect is not limited to the conduct of individuals. It also points out the mutual connections among individuals, through which the actions of a single person can have an impact on society, and in broadest terms, can change the world. Even our subtle motivations and actions can affect the whole world in a vast way. The teachings on karmic cause and effect show that we can change our lives as well as society as a whole. They show the great power that one individual has.

We tend to think of the Buddha as someone with great powers – a kind of Superman with superpowers who will come to protect us and save us when something terrible happens. But who is the real superhero? You are. Superman is not the Buddha. You are. Who is your protector? You are. What is your greatest power? It is the power of your noble motivations. Karmic cause and effect teaches us that each one of us is a person with tremendous power to change the world. Therefore, you should value yourself and trust in your own abilities. This is a key point in order to be able to take up great responsibilities, through your noble aims and intentions.

For this reason, we should not always be expecting something outside ourselves to intervene, as if we were entreating the buddhas and bodhisattvas, "Please bless me so that good things happen to me." We make continual requests to the teacher or lama to grant us their blessings. But sometimes the lama's battery is finished! So many people want to recharge from the lama that even the biggest battery can run down. There are also people who did something good in the past and now expect something good to be done to them.

I think it is very important not just to wait for the external buddhas and teachers. We also need to understand that we have an inner Buddha or an inner teacher.

That means we need to be the ones who make the effort. We need to create the opportunities, or produce the good energy, without always waiting for someone to arrive and intervene from the outside. I think it is very important to produce this by yourself, because, actually, you are the Buddha. Not such an effective buddha, perhaps, but... a buddha, a small Buddha. Our Buddha is like a child, not yet grown up enough to do more, so we need to nurture our inner Buddha, our child Buddha.

The fourth and final topic to contemplate is 'the defects of samsara'. Among the four common preliminary practices, all the topics up to this one are readily comprehensible by anyone, whether they have studied Buddhism or not. When we arrive at this topic, we encounter discussions of '*samsara*' and '*nirvana*', and these concepts require some understanding of Buddhist philosophy. However, this is not a philosophy class. I myself am not good at philosophy.

Nevertheless, we all know that we must act in certain ways to get the results we want. Everyone understands this, from tiny insects up. We all want to be happy and to avoid suffering, and we understand that we must act in certain ways to bring about those desired results. Yet we have many misunderstandings as to precisely what the causes of the desired result of happiness actually are. We mistake the causes that bring about undesirable results for causes that bring about desirable results.

In 21st-century society, many people place great emphasis on material development, in the belief that material goods will satisfy their desires and give them perfect happiness. We keep investing our energy in the consumption of material goods, recklessly and with unflagging eagerness. Yet it is exceedingly unlikely that we will ever be satisfied by the objects of our desire. No matter how much we attain, we are not satisfied. Our desires just increase, without limit, while the natural resources of our planet are subject to limitations. There is simply no way for something limited to satisfy desires that have no limit.

Since we can already foresee the big disaster that lies ahead if we continue at our current rate of consumption, now is the time for us to reflect deeply on these issues.

CHAPTER 8

NGÖNDRO II: GURU YOGA

We have briefly reviewed the four common preliminary practices. Following these come the four special preliminary practices – or, more literally, the four 'uncommon' preliminary practices. The term 'common' indicates that the practices follow the sutra presentation, whereas the term 'uncommon' or 'special' reflects the fact that these four preliminary practices are connected to the Vajrayana path. Strictly speaking, we should now discuss all four of the special preliminary practices, which comprise Refuge, Vajrasattva, Mandala Offering and Guru Yoga. However, I will be taking Guru Yoga as my main topic here.

Buddhism spread throughout Tibet from around the 7th or 8th century onwards. At that time in India, not only were the Vajrayana teachings flourishing, but also the Mahayana as well as the common or foundational teachings, also known as the Shravakayana. What came to Tibet was not limited to Vajrayana Buddhism. All three vehicles – Shravakayana, Mahayana and Vajrayana – were practised at that time in India, and the practice of all three spread within Tibet in their entirety.

There were two historical periods during which Buddhism spread in Tibet, an earlier period that was followed by a decline, and then a subsequent or later dissemination. During this subsequent spread, the Vajrayana teachings came to be practised openly and universally. The Kagyu lineage arose within this later spread of Buddhism in Tibet, as indeed did most of the four major schools found today within Tibetan Buddhism. Within the four schools, all are alike in practising guru yoga, and all place great importance on the relationship between teacher and student; or lama (or guru) and disciple.

Many of those gathered here today are disciples who met the 16th Gyalwang Karmapa and received teachings from him. The practice in Tibet of recognising reincarnations – in other words the system of reincarnation lineages – first originated with the Karmapa lineage, as is customarily explained. It was the Third Karmapa who became the first *tulku*, when he was recognised as the reincarnation of the Second Karmapa, Karma Pakshi. It was from this time that the practice of identifying reincarnations became widespread and well-known.

In order not to abandon the disciples of their previous life but continue caring for them, the lama returns as a reincarnation, or *yangsi*, and resumes the relationship with those disciples, not just for one more lifetime, but by accompanying them continuously. Therefore, after the lama passes away, the disciples search for the next reincarnation and recognise the lama in accordance with valid predictions. In that next life, the reincarnate lama then continues caring for the disciples from their previous life as their own, and will do so in the disciples' next life as well. This special relationship between lama and disciples came about through the enlightened deeds of the Karmapa, and arose through the Karmapa lineage.

As for the 16th Gyalwang Karmapa, I received the name of his reincarnation through the power of my karma. The fact that I am carrying that name through this karmic connection and now have been able to come back to Europe and meet with Karma Kagyu disciples and in particular the disciples of the 16th Gyalwang Karmapa, shows that there is a strong continuity in the relationship of lama and disciple, and an extremely wholesome and noble connection that cannot be interrupted by birth and death.

In terms of guru yoga, the relationship of teacher and student – or lama and disciple – is important in the practice of the Dharma.

Understanding how to engage in this profound relationship is an important point. It is an internal connection of the mind, not just an outer or physical connection, nor merely a matter of seeing one another or speaking together. It is an absolute connection, and a noble and wholesome one. I believe that it is very important to make this profound connection meaningful.

There are two main factors that come together to create a relationship between lama and disciple: the lama's compassion and the disciple's devotion. The lama's compassion includes affection as well as compassion, and there are many forms of affection in life, such as the affection of parents, of friends or of romantic partners.

The affection of teacher towards student is very important within the practice of the Dharma. There are some students who treat the affection of a teacher as an ordinary, worldly form of affection. Based on this attitude, thoughts arise such as, "The lama is nice to me," or, "The teacher is treating others better than me. The lama is not nice to me. The teacher taught him the Dharma, but not me." Therefore it is important to reflect carefully, to be able to recognise what the affection or compassion of a lama really is.

The teacher's love, affection and great compassion are not focused on the students' suffering merely in the form of the painful feelings that they may have. Rather, Buddhism speaks of three types of suffering. One is the suffering of painful sensations, which includes sickness and the like. A second is the suffering of change, which relates to what we usually identify as pleasant states. These pleasant feelings change to unpleasant, and ultimately turn into suffering. The third, the pervasive suffering of conditioned existence, refers not only to suffering itself, but to the fact that it comes from suffering, is caused through suffering and has suffering as its very seed or nature.

The compassion of the lama is not something temporary, arising only when we are experiencing pain. His or her concern is not just for us to feel pleasure, be physically comfortable and wealthy

– in short, to have contaminated forms of happiness. The lama's compassion does not entail seeking an increase in these visible forms of pleasure, since that would ultimately be tantamount to seeking an increase in our suffering. Rather, the compassion of the teacher is seeking to uproot our suffering completely, and destroy its seeds. We should recognise that the advice the teacher gives us is directed towards that goal, and reflect, "The lama is giving me these personal instructions in order to end my samsaric suffering and destroy the afflictive emotions and karma which are the roots of my suffering." This is an important practice.

The second key factor in the relationship between teacher and student is the devotion that comes from the student. Devotion has two meanings. One is longing, the other is respect, or aspiration. The lama should be inspiring to the disciple, as a good person or someone with exceptional or captivating qualities. Here the idea of 'captivating qualities' does not refer to the teacher's physical appearance or charisma, but to their inner, noble qualities, such as their compassion and so forth. These qualities inspire you so fully that you long to cultivate them within yourself. To that end, you respect them greatly, aspire to have them yourself and become dedicated to developing them within yourself.

This second aspect of devotion – respect – is not a matter of lavishing eloquent praises on the teacher, following some protocol or displaying external gestures of respect. In any case, each culture has its own ways of showing respect. When Westerners adopt Tibetan forms of respect, it is not very fitting somehow. Likewise when Tibetans adopt the Western forms, it does not seem very natural. No matter how well you might master the outer forms of respect, this is not the point of real respect. Rather, you can gauge how great your devotion is by the degree to which you are able to absorb the inspiring qualities of the lama into your own being, and practise them.

What is considered most important within the Kagyu lineage is for a lama to hold the lineage and possess great compassion and blessings.

Teachers first train their own minds in great compassion and wisdom, then pass the lineage of that training down, from master to disciple in successive generations, without error and without any interruption. That is the basis for the blessings, and it is the basis for the disciples to be able to practise to develop those qualities within themselves.

In this way, the lama's compassion and the disciple's devotion are the most important in the practice of the Kagyu teachings. Blessing, in turn, is precisely that. In one sense, it is a bit strange to speak of giving blessings, since there is nothing perceptible there. But if we think back instead to when we were children and remember being near our parents, we can recall a feeling of being protected and cared for – a sense of complete security. That is also a kind of blessing, I think. There is nothing to see, but through that connection or atmosphere, the child has a special feeling.

I have experienced this in my own life, when I had problems and went to see holy beings. Even though I might have had many worries and thoughts going through my mind as I was on my way to see them, when I came into their presence these naturally ceased. When I left, I would notice that, with no special effort on my part, my worries had all been eased. My mind would just naturally become relaxed, for no other reason than through the force of meeting that holy being. That is blessing.

When giving blessings, therefore, there is nothing concrete to hand over. Yet, if the lama has compassion, through its power the disciple gradually absorbs that compassion into her or himself. If that happens, you can say there was blessing. I know of no other blessing beyond that. There is no solid thing that one person gives another. Maybe someone else has some other form of blessing, but I know nothing about that.

The materialistic orientation of the 21st century has become so strong that everyone wants to instantly acquire something tangible. Because of this we lack long-term endurance and patience. We expect blessings to have the sort of instant effect that can occur when we are working with physical materials. Our attitude is, "The teacher has it and we want it, so they should hand it over to us." However, the blessings of the Dharma do not function in that way. They do not always show instant results. Sometimes it can take time. It can happen that we met a teacher three years ago, and did not feel anything special at the time. We might not even have particularly enjoyed meeting them, but three, four or five years later, when we recall that meeting, it is possible for some special feeling to arise.

In the 21st century, we have such a strong materialistic mentality that we want everything to be easy, convenient and fast. We should take care not to bring that mentality into our practice of Dharma. It does not function that way.

Sometimes when we hear the term guru yoga, the word 'yoga' leads us to expect it to involve some ritual or require us to do something specific. Rather, it is a matter of a practice that we apply to our own minds.

As for actually engaging in ngöndro practice, there is the traditional ngöndro *sadhana*, or practice text, which is the long version, and then there is a short version composed by... some mischievous person: me! The main reason I made this short ngöndro is because one year people requested me to explain the ngöndro practice, including how to do all the visualisations. However, the traditional ngöndro is very long, and I would only have three days to explain it all. I thought it would be difficult to finish even just reading the text. It occurred to me that we needed a short ngöndro and maybe in the future I could also do that short ngöndro myself, since I am a bit lazy.

Doing the short ngöndro sadhana might be beneficial for practitioners who are very busy and do not have the time to read the long sadhana. I always encourage people to do the longer, traditional one, and not to feel they should do this shorter one just because it was composed by me. I think it might be better to practise the traditional one, but you have the choice.

CHAPTER 9

MAHAMUDRA

Many people think that Tibetan Buddhism has an element of magic to it, something that can miraculously save us and solve all the problems that arise in life. This is particularly so in the case of Mahamudra. Just hearing the word, people feel excited, expecting something exotic and amazing.

It is unlikely that all problems in life will be solved because you are practising the Dharma. When people get sick, they expect the Dharma to cure their illnesses. When they face economic difficulties, they think they can increase their wealth by practising the Dharma. However, the practice of Dharma does not make all the problems in life go away, and that is not its purpose.

The practice of Dharma is aimed at eliminating our biggest or most fundamental problem in life. For that, no amount of physical health or material wealth can help. No matter how 'successful' we are, within our minds we can still feel unhappy, lonely or empty somehow. The practice of Dharma solves our mental suffering, or what we can call our un-wellness of the mind. When we reach a high level in our Dharma practice, we might attain the mental power to be able to overcome physical illnesses and other problems of that sort. But for that, our practice would need to be very advanced indeed.

Our essential aim in practising the Dharma is to create happiness and inner peace within our minds, and to transform our minds. This goal of transforming our minds lies at the very core of Dharma practice. It is the basic aim and reason for practising the Dharma, and everything else gets taken care of along the way. However, this is not to say that when you practise Dharma you should not engage in any worldly activities, or that there is no need to do so. That is not the case.

The process of transforming the mind cannot be forced. Sometimes we have problems that we are unable to face, and retreat into Dharma practice to escape those problems. Or at other times, when we have serious problems or suffering, we use our Dharma practice to try to suppress them. For instance, there are some practitioners who have issues with anger, jealousy or attachment. Since they are practising the Dharma they feel – or other people comment to them – that as Buddhist practitioners, they should not be so short-tempered or so jealous.

Thinking that you should not feel that way, instead of facing your emotions and working with the antidotes to address them, you feel ashamed and conceal your difficult emotions. If you do not deal with them but continue in this way, not only have you not rid yourself of that anger, but you have also added shame and guilt on top of that. Furthermore, you pretend that you have no anger, and show the world a calm face or a fake smile while inside you are seething. This can create mental problems. You feel you must not express what you have inside, but keep it bottled up until there is a risk of real mental illness. Or one day you just explode.

Therefore it is unhealthy to just tell yourself, "I am not allowed to have these emotions because I am a Dharma practitioner." On the other hand, expressing them indiscriminately and giving your emotions free rein is not the answer either. This just surrenders your control to them. That is why you need to learn how to work on your emotions, and take charge of them to gradually resolve them.

When we speak of applying the antidotes to the difficult emotions, this is not a matter of applying force. I have the personal experience that because I am recognised as Karmapa, in people's minds I am like the Buddha, or a god, and have no emotions. If

I showed anger, they would be shocked. They might also think I am just pretending to be angry. But sometimes I am really angry! And people either take it as a game, as if I were just pretending, or they feel mystified that the Karmapa could possibly feel anger.

People have this expectation that immediately, on the very day we become Dharma practitioners, we suddenly become a good person, a nice person. That is not the reality. In fact, sometimes as Dharma practitioners it might take us longer. In my experience, working with emotions takes a lot of time. Eliminating hatred, for instance, might take five or six years. There is no fixed period of time, but it is a long process. We need to recognise the difficult emotion or *klesha*, create a relationship to it and then enter into a sort of dialogue with it. This takes many years.

We need to get to know our emotions. Right now, they are strangers to us. When we come across them, sometimes we react as if we were being confronted by a bandit. Instead, we should make their acquaintance, and then gradually make friends with them or create a wholesome relationship with them. In the end, the fact that anger or some other emotion no longer arises is not a result of forcefully shutting it out, but a matter of very naturally or even joyfully coming to the point where you make friends with it and are naturally in control.

There is a story of a woman was not on good terms with her mother-in-law. There was constant bickering and criticising, but the wife generally tolerated it. She put up with it until she reached the point where she could not bear it any longer. She reflected that she could not escape from her mother-in-law unless she left her husband, which she did not want to do. Instead, she came to the conclusion that the only way out was to kill her.

To that end, she went to see a doctor that she was close to, to ask for some poison to use to kill her mother-in-law. This doctor gave her some advice, explaining that if the mother-in-law were to die suddenly, all the suspicion would fall on her.

The doctor told the woman, "I can give you something that will kill her, if you put it in her food every day for a year. But this will only work on one condition: you must not let her feel that you harbour any ill will towards her, so you have to treat her very well. Be gentle with her. Whatever she demands of you, do it willingly. You have to make sure she never suspects a thing. Otherwise, when she dies, people will suspect both of us."

The wife agreed, and followed these instructions. Each day she put a little of the substance she was given into the food she served her mother-in-law. At the same time, she displayed a completely different attitude towards her. She now took care to avoid entering into quarrels and took great pains to act kindly towards her. Gradually their relationship shifted, and they began to get on together very well.

Initially the woman was just pretending, but eventually the relationship changed. She and the mother-in-law both became fond of each other, to the point where she no longer wanted to kill her. However, now she had a problem. She had already given her poison. Feeling distressed, she went back to the doctor and explained that she was now getting along very well with her mother-in-law.

"I don't want to kill her any more," she told the doctor. "What can I do? Is there any antidote?"

The doctor burst out laughing, telling her, "That wasn't poison. It was just some herbs. I never gave you any poison!"

Relationships are like that, and that is the point of this story. In order to bring things under control, we need to know ourselves. If we do that, and succeed in becoming acquainted with our own minds, there will be no need to use force on our disturbing emotions. A forceful approach is not the right way.

DHARMA TEACHINGS

There is no Dharma practice that is not included within the practice of the three higher trainings. The first of these three trainings is the training in ethical conduct. Unlike other species, human beings are endowed with the capacity for moral discernment. We are capable of determining what we ought to do and what we ought not to do. This discernment must be applied as we pursue both temporary and ultimate aims. Our temporary goals involve bringing about some benefit, whereas our ultimate goal is happiness. If we take the environment as an example, because we were not taking into account the long-term goal of the well-being of the generations to come and the future of the world in general, we have committed grave errors on environmental issues as we pursued provisional and short-term comfort. These errors occurred because of a failure to distinguish between what we ought and ought not to do in terms of both temporary and ultimate aims.

For that reason, rather than consider this planet as a thing, to be dug up and used, it would be better to see her as a mother who nurtures us, her children. From generation to generation, we need this loving mother, and so must take good care of her and keep her strong and healthy.

Not only have we made errors in determining what to adopt and what to give up in pursuit of our temporary and ultimate goals; we have also made mistakes due to self-centredness. When we think only of our own individual interests, we commit serious errors in terms of what we ought to adopt or avoid for the benefit of others, as well as for our own sake.

This can happen on many different levels. For instance, in pursuit of our own interests, as individuals we ignore the well-being of others or hold them in contempt and harm them. In order to secure their own national interests, countries disdain the welfare of other countries, and act in ways that destroy their peace and happiness. The same is true of how different races and different religions behave towards one another. We human beings also destroy the habitats of other species, endanger their survival and even deprive them of their life, all for our own comfort, pleasure and profit.

This is why ethical conduct entails taking responsibility for our motivation and behaviour and applying our moral system correctly, adopting what we should adopt and avoiding what needs to be avoided.

The second higher training is the training in *samadhi*, which we can call training in meditation. One of the main reasons why many people who are practising the Dharma do not progress as they expected is because their meditation – and especially their *shamatha* and *vipashyana* meditation – is not up to the task.

With shamatha, we channel all the power of the mind to a single object, as when a stream is concentrated into a single pipe. Otherwise, as it is now, our mind is scattered and therefore its power is scattered and unfocused, with the result that our mind lacks sharpness and clarity. With shamatha we are gathering together all the power of the mind into one and concentrating it, and this gives us clarity and acuity. That is the mental power that we need to generate and apply.

In one way, the 21st century is the best time to practise shamatha. In another way, it is the worst. It is the worst because of the tremendous number of sources of entertainment and distraction. Our smartphone, the Internet and the like offer constant conditions for distraction – so much so, that some people say there is zero chance to attain shamatha nowadays. This is because a principal condition for developing shamatha is solitude. This includes both external solitude, in the form of an extended stay in physical isolation, and internal solitude, in the form of a mind free of distractions. Because of the great dependence we have on external circumstances, as beginners, we need conditions with less outer distraction in the initial phase, but those are relatively difficult to find.

On the other hand, this century is the right time to practise shamatha, because life has become so hectic and stressful, and the pressures on us have mounted so much that we have become aware of the need to calm our mind and create inner peace. It no longer seems to be optional, but urges itself on us as a necessity.

In the case of shamatha as taught within Mahamudra, it is not absolutely necessary to remain in complete solitude. When you cultivate shamatha in the context of Mahamudra, you can practise it directly in all situations in life. You practise shamatha while you walk or travel, when you are seated, and in all that you do. This is the principal approach of the practice of shamatha that is taught within Mahamudra.

Someone once asked the Third Karmapa, Rangjung Dorje, whether he had any instructions that would allow a person to become enlightened without having to meditate. "If you have any," this man said, "please give me them."

In one way, this is a stupid question, and shows great arrogance, thinking you can reach enlightenment without meditating. But Rangjung Dorje told him, "Yes, I do. But if I give it to you, it won't help you, because no matter how much I tell you not to meditate, you will try to cultivate something and will be meditating. No matter how much I tell you to leave your mind unaltered in its natural state – not to force anything but just relax – you will be altering your mind trying to reach that state. So these instructions won't help you."

Even though we can say of Mahamudra meditation that there is no need to meditate and nothing to alter, we cannot understand this, because we are always looking to do something. This is the problem. We all know that the human mind is what we sometimes call a 'monkey mind'. It is so restless that we are accustomed to being disturbed, and are always analysing or engaging mentally with something or other. This is why, even if our teacher tells us, "With this practice, you do not need to do anything. Just relax and be with yourself," still we do not relax. Our minds are never at ease.

Maybe we think this approach is too easy. Why do we find it so difficult to do this meditation practice? Is it because it is too difficult? Or because it is too easy? I think the answer is: too easy. That is why we do not know how to do it.

Mahamudra practice involves gradually shifting away from our strong habits of altered and restless states until we are able to rest without trying to change or fabricate anything, just letting ourselves be as we are, naturally. This is how we need to habituate our minds instead.

Although there are numerous methods for training in shamatha, many masters prefer those that use the breath as an object of focus. This is because breathing is something we are constantly doing anyway. Our breath is not something that is only present when we are meditating and not otherwise. Therefore when we focus on the breath, we do not need to do anything special or create anything new. We simply place the mind on what is naturally already there. Instead of thinking that practice involves doing something out of the ordinary, we just return to or settle into what is already happening. That is why the breath is taken as an object of meditation.

However, sometimes people then think that breathing meditation means inhaling very deeply, holding their breath for a bit and then blowing all the air out of their lungs. I think this happens precisely because they think, "I am meditating. I should be doing something special or unusual." But they have forgotten that they are already breathing. We have this problem of always wanting to do something intentionally. There is no need to intentionally breathe. Just relax on your breathing. Be aware of the breath. That is all.

I also have this problem. Sometimes the doctor comes and says, "I'm going to give you an injection. Just relax." As soon as he tells me this, I am no longer relaxed. It would be better to tell me, "Don't relax." That might be more relaxing! Even the word 'relax' can make us more tense. It puts pressure on us to relax.

When we are trying to focus our mind and take a thought or perception as our object of attention, one challenge we face is that when a new thought arises we cannot keep our mind focused on the first thought. When we try but fail to hold on to the first thought, we become shaken by that, and feel upset. In fact, there is no need to feel upset by this. Whenever a new thought comes, let it come. It does not matter if you could not keep your mind focused on the earlier thought. Thoughts will arise one after the other, and as they do, you just keep resting your awareness on the thoughts as they pass by.

Generally shamatha and vipashyana must be practised in this order – first shamatha and only after that, vipashyana, like cause and effect. However, in Mahamudra there exists a practice that unites shamatha and vipashyana. In the classical treatises there are precise definitions and standards for measuring shamatha and vipashyana, but rather than enter into these complicated discussions, I thought it might be better to discuss the actual practice of unified shamatha and vipashyana.

In this practice, when an emotional thought of anger arises, for example, we do not particularly need to block it or have concerns about it. Nor do we need to follow the thought, or accompany it. In this context, alertness and mindfulness have great importance. We are simply aware of the nature of that thought, or what we might describe as the situation of that thought, and remain mindful of it. However, this does not imply that we launch an investigation into the nature of that thought. We just observe the image of the thought, or its shape, so to speak. We are not analysing or seeking to determine what the nature of thought is, whether it is emptiness or not. We just look at it.

When you manage to do that, if the thought is a disturbing emotion, it loses its basis of support in the truth. Since the emotion lacks a source and a reason, its strength gradually diminishes. This is similar to when a person who is telling lies is found out. When we discover that what they said had no basis in truth, the person either slips away out of embarrassment or becomes diminished.

This is why, when a negative emotion arises, there is no need to feel nervous or afraid. Just look at its nature. Be aware of the situation. That negative emotion is like a person telling lies, because there is no truth behind it, nor is it based in reason. Therefore when you look at it, it is as if the negative emotion becomes ashamed of itself and weakens. It becomes smaller. This is not a technique to completely uproot the disturbing emotions, but it will help.

This is what is called the practice of unified shamatha and vipashyana. While the mind is at peace as it rests in a state of equipoise, the power of alertness and mindfulness becomes manifest. Through their power, you recognise the nature of the thoughts that arise.

These comments are regarding the higher training in meditation, which is the second of the three higher trainings. The third is the higher training in wisdom, which is what eradicates the disturbing emotions completely and is the method that allows us to actually understand their nature. When we speak of wisdom, we should not think solely in terms of philosophy or of intellectual understanding. Rather it is something to be experienced directly – realised and seen directly. I do not particularly have anything more to say about wisdom.

Regarding Mahamudra, most of you are students of the 16th Gyalwang Karmapa or of Kagyu lamas who themselves are students of the 16th Gyalwang Karmapa and for whom I myself have devotion and respect. That makes me junior to you, so it is not very fitting for me to be speaking to you about Mahamudra, pretending that I actually know something about it. Nevertheless, I have made this effort to say something.

However, it is important to understand that Mahamudra realisations cannot be produced by applying our ordinary efforts or by sheer hard work, as if it were any other task or an ordinary job. We need an extraordinary power and effort. The main point is this: it is said that when the teacher's compassion and student's devotion come together, Mahamudra realisations are easily attained.

To that end, we will next have an 84 Mahasiddha Empowerment. The 84 Mahasiddhas all attained great *siddhis* – or spiritual attainments – through the meeting of the teacher's compassion with the student's devotion. However, in Tibetan Buddhism and especially in Vajrayana practices, the lama can become an object of fear and danger to the disciple. The teacher can appear wrathful... really! At any rate, some fear comes to be associated with the teacher, and students do feel pressure as a result, either because the teacher inspires the fear or because the students themselves generate it. I think there are misunderstandings here. As it is described in the biographies of earlier masters, it is important for us to see our lama as a close spiritual friend – a trusted friend and our best friend. We should not see them as just any sort of friend, since there are many sorts of friends, such as drinking buddies – alcoholic friends! The lama is not that sort of friend, but a virtuous friend who accompanies us in the direction of virtue, on whom we can rely completely – a wonderful friend.

We have excellent examples from the past of teachers and students working together closely, almost every day. In ancient times, students mostly stayed with their teacher, meeting daily for some sort of discussion or to report in. It was not a matter of the teacher seated high on the throne demanding that the student promise to do various things. Rather, the teacher almost becomes another face of yourself, no longer another person but part of you – part of your mind or part of your heart, you could say.

This is very important, but these days we can have problems with this when the teacher is somewhere in Asia and the student is somewhere in Europe. However, sometimes even when there is no such physical distance, there might still be little real connection. The external closeness is less important than the inner closeness, therefore this should be our outlook towards the teacher-student relationship. It should not be a complicated or fearful relationship.

PART THREE

TEACHINGS DURING EMPOWERMENTS

NÜRBURGRING AND BERLIN

CHAPTER 10

84 Mahasiddha Empowerment

The reason we speak of 84 *mahasiddhas* – or greatly accomplished masters – is that at one point, there were 84 mahasiddhas who gathered together at a single time to hold a *ganachakra* feast, which is something like a party. This does not mean there were only 84 mahasiddhas in India. In fact, there were countless enlightened and accomplished masters in India and in Tibet, and in other countries as well. I think there have also been many unknown accomplished masters in the West.

While I was in Tibet, Situ Rinpoche and Gyaltsab Rinpoche came twice, but just for a short time, so they did not have the opportunity to confer much in the way of transmissions. I used to feel embarrassed when I was very young that I could not grant any really complicated empowerments, as other lamas did. I could only repeat the same one or two simple empowerments over and over. Of course, that is nothing to be embarrassed about, but I used to think how nice it would be to be able to give a big, impressive empowerment. This is how a child thinks. Actually, some attendants had suggested to me that I should confer something more than the simple empowerments I was giving. But how could I, since I did not have the lineage transmission for them? When I was very young, before I was recognised as Karmapa, I had visited the seat of Situ Rinpoche – Palpung Monastery in Kham – while Rinpoche was there. Palpung is far from my home-town, but I think we travelled there mainly because my family thought I was someone special. They used to tell me of all the auspicious signs that appeared when I was born, but there was a lingering uncertainty as to precisely who I was – that is to say, which tulku. It never occurred to us that I was Karmapa. That was too high. But my father took me to see Situ Rinpoche to try to find out who I was.

At that time Situ Rinpoche conferred many important and complex empowerments, among which was the 84 Mahasiddha Empowerment. I was seated in the assembly with others, but since I was five or six years old, it was out of the question for me to do the visualisations. I was also a bit naughty, running back and forth. It is rather doubtful that I actually received the empowerments, but I was emboldened and told myself boastfully that I could probably consider that I had received the 84 Mahasiddha Empowerment. Subsequent to that, before I left Tibet, I decided to give that empowerment. It is not such a simple empowerment, you see – after all, there is not just one deity; there are 84 mahasiddhas! At that time, I had a boost of confidence and thought I would confer a big empowerment, so I gave this one, twice. Now I will do it again today.

Prior to that, since some people have requested to receive the refuge vows, as part of the preparation for the empowerment I will first give the refuge vows – it does not seem quite right to call this a vow ceremony, since there will be very little that is ceremonial to it!

When we fall sick, if we have a minor illness, we might conceivably find a way to treat it ourselves. But if our illness is serious, we look for qualified doctors, and take care that we are treated in good hospitals with high-quality medicines and properly trained nursing staff. By bringing together all the right conditions in this way, we have a much greater chance of being cured.

Similarly, if we are to free ourselves from the sufferings of samsara along with their causes, we need to rely on the Three Jewels as our source of refuge. Going for refuge does not mean simply placing our hope and trust in the Three Jewels; in the same way that a sick person needs to receive treatment, so we too need to practise the Dharma.

CHAPTER 11

VAJRASATTVA

Vajrasattva practice is said to be the most effective method for purifying any transgression of the three types of vow (*pratimoksha*, *bodhisattva* or *tantra*). There is a difference between engaging in a wrong-doing such as killing, on the one hand, versus killing while holding the commitment not to kill, on the other hand. Of course, in both cases, there is wrong-doing, which has its own negative effect, but killing with the additional element of violating a commitment not to do so has a stronger effect on your mind.

What we seek to purify with this practice are all the negative deeds committed since beginningless time. As Buddhists, we accept the existence of past and future lives. This entails a continuation of consciousness from life to life. All the positive or negative actions we carry out leave an impression on our consciousness, and this continues on. We could describe this impression as a sort of energy.

Astronomy and cosmic science are still debating the origins of the cosmos and argue various theories involving a Big Bang, a single atom and so forth. There are still many difficulties in positing a beginning to the cosmos. Similarly, in the case of the continuation of consciousness, there are many difficulties in positing a beginning point, and thus consciousness is explained to be beginningless. When we are purifying, we purify all the negative deeds accumulated through all our lives since beginningless time, whether we are aware of having done them or not. Thus when we are confessing for purification, we call on the Buddhas and bodhisattvas as our witnesses. Since later in life we do not recall all the misdeeds we have committed earlier in life, it is clear that we are not aware of all that we have done. Therefore, we freely confess everything that those who have the eyes of wisdom can see and know we have done.

When confessing for purification, the most important point is that you regret what you have done and make a firm resolve not to repeat it in the future. The effectiveness of the purification depends on the four opponent powers – the support (or reliance), regret, remedy (or antidote) and resolve – and within those four the powers of regret and resolve are the most important.

There is also a key distinction to be made between a person and their actions. The person's action may have been wrong and faulty, but the person acted as they did because they had fallen under the sway of a klesha, or disturbing emotion, and therefore lost control of themselves. The action is faulty and blameworthy, but the person is neither faulty nor blameworthy. When we are generating regret, we must keep this distinction in mind.

In the course of engaging in purification practice, I feel it is important to make a separation or put some distance between oneself and one's misdeeds. Without that, many people who do something wrong become weighed down by their mistakes and feel that they are eternally guilty. I know some people who feel so guilty and have so much negative energy in their mind that they cannot lift themselves up from what you could call that dark energy. Therefore we need to put some distance between ourselves and the negative things we have done.

To that end, we need to have a clear understanding that the reason that we committed those negative acts is because we were under the control of disturbing or negative emotions, very much like a person who has a mental problem or mental illness. Although we do not usually consider this to be a mental problem, actually it is a big problem. Sometimes I have this strong feeling that when I got angry I became a different person. When I recall those situations, I even feel a bit afraid of myself, because I feel as though I do not know that person and I wonder who that dangerous person was.

This understanding – that there is a distinction between person and action – should not be applied only to ourselves, but also to other people. If we are practising patience, then when others do harmful things to us, we need to think very carefully and clearly about why they act in that way. We might normally become very angry or think that someone has been very bad to us, but actually we need to understand that the person has come under the control of negative emotions. A good example is when a person takes a stick and beats us. We do not feel anger towards the stick; we recognise that the stick is innocent, because it is controlled by the person. Similarly, a person acting out of anger is like that stick. The negative emotion uses the person, just like a hand uses a stick. It is the emotion that controls the situation, therefore we need to keep clear this differentiation between a person and their actions.

When purifying, along with feeling regret for our own past misdeeds, we make a firm resolve to refrain from those actions in the future. Some people have problems with this because they think it would be inconsistent to undertake this resolution if there is a chance that they might break their commitment and repeat the action in the future. This should not prevent us from making the resolve. If we do fall and make a mistake, it is fine simply to generate a fresh resolve.

CHAPTER 12

MEDICINE BUDDHA

Traditional Tibetan medicine is connected to the Buddhadharma. In identifying the causes of a disease, the Tibetan science of healing speaks of two types: proximate causes and ultimate, or long-term, causes. When we contract a physical disease, we find conditions that are close to us or immediate, and these are what are described as proximate causes. For example, when a doctor examines us, he or she might find an imbalance of the elements in the body, or harmful bacteria.

Tibetan medical science explains that if we analyse more deeply, we also find ultimate or long-term causes for the disease. These are connected to the mind, and include such disturbing emotional states as anger, attachment and ignorance. When analysing the causes and conditions for disease, healing and good health, Tibetan medicine is very attentive to interdependence – that is to say, to the way in which different factors are interrelated and impact upon one another. This approach is not primarily one where physicians locate harmful bacteria or tumours, and remove them. Rather, the Tibetan science of healing considers it important to take into account the interrelationships among the many parts of the body, and the way that one condition is connected to many others.

Today's society is one of tremendous stress, where most people are under great pressure of different sorts. This stress forms a condition that results in many emotional problems and what we can call psychological problems or mental illness. To go beyond the temporary relief of this pain and direct our efforts to creating lasting peace and happiness within the mind, it is not enough to just take pills. The mind has to give itself appropriate medicine – mental medicine. To bring about mental peace and happiness, it is important to apply a mental cure.

CHAPTER 13

KARMA PAKSHI

The mahasiddha, or great accomplished master, Karma Pakshi, is usually considered to be the second Karmapa. However, he was actually the first to bear the name 'Karmapa', since it was only during the time of Karma Pakshi that the name Karmapa became widely known to the public. This is why one of the epithets for Karma Pakshi is 'The One Widely Known as Karmapa'. Strictly speaking, therefore, Karma Pakshi ought to be considered the first Karmapa.

However, the first in the lineage known as the 'Bearer of the Black Crown' was Düsum Khyenpa, as it was he who had the vision of a black crown, and who then wore a crown in accordance with that vision. The Black Crown seems to have existed in the time of Düsum Khyenpa. Therefore, Düsum Khyenpa was identified as the first in the reincarnation lineage of the Bearer of the Black Crown. Later, however, the Karmapa and the Bearer of the Black Crown came to be considered inseparable, and they were no longer counted as distinct.

Historians differ as to how the name 'Karmapa' arose. Some scholars say that Karma Pakshi earned the name due to the great amount of time he spent at Karma Monastery, in the area called Karma. However, according to eminent scholars of the Karma Kamtsang lineage, 'Karmapa' had been the secret name of Düsum Khyenpa. The name became public during the time of Karma Pakshi, but Düsum Khyenpa himself had gained it during a vision in which he was enthroned as the one who performs the enlightened activity of all the buddhas.

Similarly the name of the Third Karmapa, Rangjung Dorje, had initially been the secret name of Karma Pakshi, but became a public name only subsequently, in the time of Rangjung Dorje. Likewise the Fourth Karmapa's name, Rölpe Dorje, had been the secret name of the Third Karmapa, Rangjung Dorje, and became a public name only later during the life of his successor.

Karma Pakshi was unique in the Karmapa reincarnation lineage. He was born into a line of yogis holding a Nyingma secret mantra lineage, and thus he had a connection to Nyingma. Later, he received Mahamudra instructions from Bomdrakpa, a disciple of Düsum Khyenpa's direct disciple who was named Drogön Sangye Rechen. In this way, he was someone who engaged in the unified practice of Dzogchen and Mahamudra, and the older and later tantras.

When the great master Padmasambhava came to Tibet, he displayed many miracles in order to tame humans and non-humans. Similarly, Karma Pakshi was invited by the Mongolian emperor to China, where he too performed many miracles. In that way, he was a powerful lama who directly displayed great miraculous power.

There is a recording of a Karma Pakshi empowerment that the 16th Gyalwang Karmapa gave in Europe, and I have listened to it many times. So I am pretending to be like him, in giving this empowerment on my first trip here.

The drum I have been using during this empowerment is said to have been used by Karma Pakshi, and belonged to Jamyang Khyentse Chökyi Lodrö. It was lent for use in this empowerment by Sogyal Rinpoche in his great kindness, and I think this is exceptionally auspicious.

PART FOUR

WORDS OF THANKS

CHAPTER 14

NÜRBURGRING

We have come to the conclusion of the programme organised by the Kamalashila Institute. This is the first time I have had the opportunity to come to Europe. Previously we were far apart. I was unable to come here, and it was difficult for you to come to me. Although this time I could not visit other countries, many people from neighbouring countries have been able to come to Germany. This was an excellent opportunity, and it has worked out very well.

Many of my friends here have been waiting a long time for me to come to Europe. I was also waiting and hoping for this to happen. I think it was the fact that we kept our hope stable over all these years that I was, in the end, able to come. This demonstrates that the hope we kept alive for so many years had great strength, and has not gone to waste.

The Indian government played a vital role in my being able to come here today. Some of my friends within the government worked particularly hard to make this possible, and although they are not here today for me to thank personally, I would like to take this opportunity to express my deepest appreciation and gratitude to them.

His Holiness the Dalai Lama and the Central Tibetan Administration consistently provided tremendous support, from the start right through to the end. Without their help and support, there would have been no hope of my coming here, no matter how much I might have wished to. I am extremely grateful to them as well.

The German government, central as well as state, has been of great help.

The various Dharma centres and many individuals came together and joined their efforts, and what has resulted from that is a great and worthy cause for rejoicing. We can rejoice together in our own efforts, and in the efforts of one another.

Finally, I want to express deep thanks to all the volunteers. Thank you for your sincere motivation.

Once again, thanks to you all, and see you again!

CHAPTER 15

BERLIN

This has been my first opportunity to visit Europe, and I would like to express my delight, and thank the various Kagyu Dharma centres that organised this trip, as well as the non-Kagyu centres who worked on the trip, and I especially thank the Karma Kagyu Trust.

The fact that I was able to come here today is thanks to the Government of India, as well as the Central Tibetan Administration. Without their support and endorsement, I would have been utterly unable to come here today, and I am deeply grateful to them for that. Similarly the German government lent its support directly and indirectly, so I would like to take this occasion to offer thanks to all those involved in making it possible for me to come here. This has been the cause of much happiness and boundless joy for many people, as is very apparent, and this in turn gives me great joy.

Most important are the Dharma friends in the various European countries. It is because of you that I have come here. You are the main reason. You have been waiting for many years with great patience, and I thank you for that. I apologise for all the time that you had to wait.

Through our pure altruistic intentions, pure faith and pure sacred bond of *samaya*, we have gathered together here in a single mandala. This is something very fortunate that makes me feel I have accomplished something vast and of great significance in life, and I feel very happy about that. I rejoice deeply and want to express my gratitude to all of you and to your friends.

I especially want to say thank you very much to all the volunteers. I will remember forever your sincere motivation and dedication, and your hard work.

People from many different Dharma centres from all over Europe have gathered here, and I would like to say that the most important thing is to have harmony and to connect and work closely together. Buddha Shakyamuni said the thing that would destroy his Dharma would be conflict among the holders of his teachings. The actual cause of its destruction will be conflict and lack of harmony. It is very important that, even if we do not become holders of the teachings, we at least do not become harmers of the teachings.

The history of the past few decades has given us in the Karma Kagyu some hard lessons in this. These should serve as a reminder to us of the need to train in pure view and to guard the purity of our mutual sacred bonds. If we are able to do this, we will fulfil the wishes of the 16th Gyalwang Karmapa.

As for when I will come back to Europe, it is hard to say. It could be soon, it could be in three or four years, or it could be some other time. But as I said earlier, since my childhood I have kept you in mind and heart. You are all in my heart and mind, very close. I have said many prayers and made a great effort to come here, and want you to know that I hold you in my mind and heart, and that we will never be separate.

I continually pray for your life to be a meaningful life, and a happy one.

About the Author

As the spiritual head of the 900-year-old Karma Kagyu lineage of Tibetan Buddhism, His Holiness the 17th Karmapa, Ogyen Trinley Dorje, has emerged as an important thought-leader for our time. Since his dramatic escape from Tibet to India in 2000, the Karmapa has played a key role in preserving Tibetan religion and culture. The Karmapa has been described as 'a world spiritual leader for the 21st century', and has inspired millions of people worldwide to take action on social and environmental issues. At the age of 29, the Karmapa's message has particularly resonated with young people, whom he encourages to take on the responsibility to create a more compassionate future for the planet.

'Karmapa' literally means 'He Who Performs the Activities of the Buddha' and the Karmapa lineage itself is known for putting Buddhist principles into action. The Khoryug association that he founded in 2009 has transformed over 55 monasteries across the Himalayas into local centres for environmental activism. Leading on women's issues, in January 2015 His Holiness the 17th Karmapa made the historic announcement that he will establish full ordination for women, a long-awaited step within Tibetan Buddhism.

The Karmapa receives thousands of visitors annually at his residence in northern India, and discusses practical global solutions with people from all around the world. His Holiness the Karmapa engages in a wide range of artistic activities. He paints, draws calligraphy, writes poetry, creates theatrical events and composes music.

———

The 17th Karmapa, Ogyen Trinley Dorje, was born in 1985 to a family of nomads in the remote highlands of the Tibetan plateau. He spent the first seven years of his life in a pristine environment free of all modern conveniences including electricity and motor vehicles. Living close to the earth, he and his tightly knit family shifted camp with the changing seasons as they cared for their herds of sheep and yak.

When he was seven, a search party for the reincarnation of the 16th Karmapa arrived in the remote valley where his family was camped. After careful comparison of the details of the boy's family and birthplace with predictions and a letter left by the 16th Karmapa, the party declared that they had found the 17th Karmapa. At this point, the young Karmapa left this nomadic lifestyle behind and made the first major journey of his life, travelling to the distant Tsurphu Monastery, the main monastic seat where every single Karmapa in the 900-year-old lineage has lived, for at least some part of his life.

In Tsurphu, he was formally enthroned as the 17th Karmapa, with two of the three living heads of his lineage officiating. Soon thereafter he commenced the traditional process of training and preparation to assume his responsibilities as Karmapa. He delivered his first public religious discourse at Tsurphu, to an audience of over 20,000 people, at the age of eight.

In the years to come, the Karmapa would face numerous challenges in his efforts to perform his spiritual activities. At the age of 14, his concern that he would be unable to fulfil his responsibilities as Karmapa in Tibet led him to the decision to escape to India. One night, during the final days of the 20th century, the teenage Karmapa leapt from an upstairs window of the monastery to join a few close aides, thus beginning a perilous journey of escape. The small party fled across the Himalayas to India, travelling under cover of darkness, at times by jeep, on horseback, on foot and by helicopter.

On January 5, 2000, the Karmapa reached Dharamsala in Northern India, and his escape from Tibet instantly made world news. Upon arrival, he was received personally by His Holiness the Dalai Lama, with whom he enjoys a close relationship of mentor and protégé to this day. The Karmapa was soon offered temporary quarters at nearby Gyuto Monastery, where he continues to reside even now. He soon resumed his traditional monastic training and philosophical education, while also taking up studies of modern subjects including science, English and other languages.

In 2004, His Holiness assumed responsibility for the Kagyu Monlam, an annual gathering to make aspiration prayers in Bodhgaya, the site where the Buddha was enlightened. Under his guidance, this annual event has grown to over 12,000 participants from all over the globe, and is watched worldwide online by tens of thousands of people.

In his pioneering role as founder and chair of the Khoryug environmental association, the Karmapa has educated thousands of monks and nuns, mobilising them to lead their local communities on environmental issues and to implement numerous projects in and around their monasteries and nunneries.

A leader for the new century, His Holiness the Karmapa makes effective use of technology to transmit and teach the Dharma widely. When he delivered a talk at a TED conference in Bangalore in 2009, he was the youngest speaker ever to have done so. His teachings are often webcast live with translation into a dozen languages. Within his own school of Tibetan Buddhism, he has been modernising religious practices, yet remains firmly rooted in tradition as he re-invigorates monastic discipline in his lineage.

Preserving and renewing Tibetan artistic forms, the Karmapa has written and produced several plays that combine elements of traditional Tibetan opera and modern theatre. His first play, a drama on the life of the great Tibetan yogi Milarepa, drew an audience of 20,000 people for its first performance, in 2010 in Bodhgaya, India.

Since 2011, he has engaged with groups of university students and young people from Europe and North America, and, most recently, with Tibetans studying in Indian universities. In 2014, the Karmapa Foundation Europe arranged for a group of 16 young professionals from across Europe to spend two weeks in India in daily dialogue with the Karmapa on issues ranging from leadership to addiction to conflict resolution. His last book, *The Heart Is Noble: Changing the World from the Inside Out*, was based on a series of such conversations with university students on the major challenges facing society today, including gender issues, food justice, rampant consumerism, and the environmental crisis.

In 2014, His Holiness the Karmapa made his first long-awaited trip to Europe. During his visit, along with giving the teachings presented in this book, the Karmapa also joined the Vespers service at a Benedictine abbey, was received by the Archdiocese of Cologne, met with the Rabbi Ben-Chorin of Berlin and paid his respects at the Holocaust Monument.

In 2015, the 17th Karmapa committed to taking the first step in establishing *bhikshuni* ordination for nuns within Tibetan Buddhism. In 2014, the Karmapa had already instituted an annual Arya Kshema Winter Dharma Gathering for Karma Kagyu nuns extending access to rigorous education for nuns, and arranging for empowerment initiatives in the nunneries.

OTHER PUBLICATIONS BY THE 17TH KARMAPA

The Heart Is Noble
Changing the World from the Inside Out

The Future Is Now
Timely Advice for Creating a Better World

Traveling the Path of Compassion
A Commentary on the Thirty-Seven Practices of a Bodhisattva

Ngondro for our Current Day
A Short Ngondro Practice and its Instructions

CPSIA information can be obtained
at www.ICGtesting.com
Printed in the USA
LVOW12s0329090617

537508LV00001B/174/P